Animal  Lives

FROGS AND TOADS

Sally Morgan

QED Publishing

Copyright © QED Publishing 2008

First published in the UK in 2008 by
QED Publishing
A Quarto Group company
226 City Road
London EC1V 2TT

www.qed-publishing.co.uk

A Catalogue record for this book is
available from the British Library.

ISBN 978 1 84835 026 7

Written by Sally Morgan
Design and editorial by East River Partnership

Publisher Steve Evans
Creative Director Zeta Davies

Printed and bound in China

Picture Credits

Key: t = top, b = bottom, l = left, r = right,
c = centre, FC = front cover

Corbis /Michael & Patricia Fogden 5b, /David
A. Northcott 8–9, /Jean Hall: Cordaiy Photo
Library Ltd 13t, /Michael & Patricia Fogden 17r;
Ecoscene /Papilio/Robert Pickett 4–5, /Papilio/
Paul Franklin 4bl, /Papilio/Robert Pickett 11,
/Papilio/Robert Pickett 12–13, /Papilio/Robert
Pickett 13b, /Papilio/Robert Pickett 14, /Papilio/
Robert Pickett 15, /Papilio/Robert Pickett 16–17,
/Papilio/Robert Pickett 22–23, /Papilio/David
Manning 23t, /Papilio/Robert Pickett 25br,
/Papilio/Paul Franklin 28–29, /Alan Beatty
29b, /Papilio/Robert Pickett 30br; **Photoshot/
NHPA** /Joe Blossom 7t, /Stephen Dalton
20–21, /Daniel Heuclin 21br; **Shutterstock** /Lynn
Watson Background, /Phil Morley 1, /Tom C
Amon 6–7, /Dr Morley Read 7b, /Graham@
theGraphicZone 10, /Elemental Imaging 16b,
/Sosnin Michael Aleksandrovich 18, /Chin Kit
Sen 19, /John Arnold 24–25, /Ecoprint 26,
/Joseph 27, /Wolfgang Staib 30m, /Graham@
theGraphicZone 30tr, /Quayside 30bl.

Words in **bold** are explained
in the Glossary on page 31.

Contents

Amphibians

Frogs and toads are amphibians. An amphibian is an animal that lives both on land and in water. The word amphibian comes from the Greek words *amphi*, which means 'both', and *bios*, which means 'life'. Newts and salamanders, like frogs and toads, are also amphibians.

Frog or toad?

Most frogs have smooth, moist skin and long back legs, which they use for leaping. Toads, on the other hand, have drier, more bumpy skin and shorter back legs, which are better for crawling. Neither frogs nor toads have tails.

Frogs are found in damp places as they have a moist skin that loses water easily.

The cane toad can grow to be the size of a football.

Most frogs, like this tree frog, have a wide mouth and bulging eyes.

Metamorphosis

The life cycle of a frog or toad starts with a tiny egg. This grows into a **larva** called a tadpole, which then changes into an adult frog or toad. This change in appearance is called **metamorphosis**.

Frog and toad fact!

The goliath frog, at up to 34 centimetres long, is the world's largest frog. At less than 2 centimetres long, the smallest is the Cuban pygmy frog.

5

Tadpoles

The eggs of frogs and toads hatch into tiny larvae called tadpoles. These tadpoles have a small, oval body and a long tail.

Gills and legs

When it first hatches, a tadpole uses feathery **gills** on the outside of its body to breathe underwater. After a while, these gills disappear and the tadpole starts to breathe through new gills inside its body. As it gets bigger, the tadpole grows two back legs, then two front legs.

Feeding

Young tadpoles first feed on plants and **algae** in the water. As they get older, tadpoles catch and eat small insects.

The back legs of the tadpole of a common frog appear after about eight weeks.

The eggs of the common frog hatch after about 12 days. Eggs from tree frogs hatch after only two days.

This common frog tadpole is about 12 weeks old and now has four legs.

Leaving water

A tadpole's body changes as it becomes a young frog or toad. Its body becomes slimmer and its backbone sticks out. The tail gets shorter until it disappears. The head also changes. The mouth becomes wider, while the eyes get rounder and bulge out. Inside, the gills are replaced by lungs that can breathe air. Once this happens, the young frog or toad is ready to crawl on to land.

This young frog, or 'froglet', is about three months old. It now has lungs and is ready to leave its pond.

Enemies of the tadpole

Tadpoles have to face many dangers, so it is not surprising that only a few survive to become adult frogs or toads. A large number are eaten by birds, such as ducks, and insects, including dragonflies and beetles. Disease also kills tadpoles, and some will die because the water in their pond dries up.

Frog and toad fact!

Some tree frogs in the rainforest lay their eggs in tiny pools of water trapped by plant leaves. The tadpoles live in these pools until they have changed into little froglets.

This diving beetle has caught a tadpole.

15

Frog and toad senses

Frogs and toads find food by using their senses, especially their senses of sight and smell.

Detecting vibrations

Frogs and toads do not have ears that stick out of their head. Instead, their ears are round and lie on the surface of their head behind each eye. Frogs and toads can hear well on land and in water. Their ears can also feel tiny vibrations in water.

Frogs have eyelids to keep their eyes moist and clear from dust and dirt.

Seeing in all directions

Frogs and toads have large, round eyes that turn easily. This means that they are able to see clearly in all directions and watch out for predators creeping up from behind! Frogs and toads also see in 3D. This means that they can tell how far away their **prey** is before they leap to catch it.

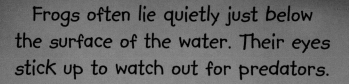

Frogs often lie quietly just below the surface of the water. Their eyes stick up to watch out for predators.

Smells in the air

Frogs and toads do not use their nose to smell. Instead, they have a sense organ in the roof of their mouth to do this.

Frog and toad fact!

Frogs and toads find their way back to their breeding ponds by smelling the air. Each pond has its own smell.

Frog and toad food

Frogs and toads are predators. This means that they hunt and eat animals and insects. Their prey includes spiders, earthworms and even other frogs and toads.

Sticky tongues

To catch a small insect, a frog or toad flicks out its long tongue and traps the insect on its sticky surface. It then pulls in its tongue and swallows the insect whole. This process takes only a fraction of a second.

Frog and toad fact!
The crab-eating frog is found in the salty waters of mangrove swamps in Southeast Asia.

Wide mouth

Frogs and toads can eat quite large prey as their mouth is wide. Once inside their mouth, small, backward facing teeth prevent prey from escaping. Frogs and toads do not chew their food. Instead, they swallow it whole by closing their mouth and pressing down on the food with their eyeballs!

This tree frog is just about to flick out its tongue to catch an insect.

This huge goliath frog has caught a smaller frog and is trying to push it into its wide mouth.

Frog and toad enemies

Frogs and toads eat small animals and insects, but they are themselves eaten by larger predators. Their enemies include birds, **mammals**, **reptiles** and fish.

Frog and toad fact!

To protect itself, the common toad makes itself look larger and more fierce by standing on tiptoes and puffing up its body.

Lying in wait

Tree frogs, for example, are hunted by snakes that lie silently in branches waiting for their prey to pass by. Some bats eat frogs, too. At night, they fly down and snatch tree frogs off leaves.

This ornate horned frog has puffed up its body to look bigger.

This green-headed tree snake has caught a frog, which it will swallow whole.

Danger in the water

Frogs swimming in water are in danger from birds, such as herons and egrets. These birds stand at the edge of a pond or river ready to catch any passing frogs with their sharp beaks. Some fish also eat frogs. The pike, for example, hides in water plants ready to pounce on any frogs that swim close to its powerful jaws.

Frog and toad defences

Frogs and toads have many ways to defend themselves from their predators. The poison arrow frogs of South America, for example, produce a highly poisonous liquid that they ooze through their skin. Even a tiny amount of this is enough to kill a person. Poison arrow frogs are brightly coloured to warn other animals to leave them alone.

Frog and toad fact!

Some South American rainforest tribes smear the tips of their arrows with a powerful poison taken from the poison arrow frog. This is how the frog got its name.

The colourful poison arrow frog produces one of the most deadly substances made by any animal.

Hidden from sight

Some frogs and toads use **camouflage** to hide from their predators. Leaf frogs, for example, are coloured or shaped to look like leaves on the ground. Other frogs look as if they are covered in moss. Camouflage also helps frogs and toads to catch their prey, as they can wait for prey to pass close by without being seen.

This frog looks just like a piece of moss on a tree trunk.

Communication

The call of the painted reed frog sounds like a shrill whistle.

Frogs and toads are small but very noisy animals! They make lots of sounds, including duck-like croaks, trills, grunts and whistles. Each species can be identified by its call.

Frogs and toads have vocal chords in their throat, just like people. They produce a sound by changing the shape of their throat and forcing air through the vocal chords. They make this sound much louder by inflating a pouch under their throat.

Male chorus

Most frogs make their calls at night when sounds travel further. These calls can sometimes be heard up to one kilometre away. The noise is especially loud when the male frogs in a group, known as a 'chorus', call together.

The coqui frog makes its mating croak at night and does not stop until the sun rises.

Frog and toad fact!

The deafening croak of the male coqui frog, which is found in the rainforests of Puerto Rico, can be as loud as the noise from a chain saw or a pneumatic drill.

Calling to females

A male calls to attract a female. Sometimes, however, the call can be a warning to other males to stay away. Females make sounds, too, but their calls are much quieter.

Frogs and toads under threat

Frogs and toads are under threat all around the world. The biggest problem comes from the loss of their habitats, the places where they live. For example, large areas of rainforest are being cleared and many ponds, where frogs and toads breed, are being drained. Changes in the weather and pollution from farms and factories are also having a bad effect on their habitats.

New ponds

Frogs and toads can be helped by making new ponds in gardens, in parks and in the countryside. Special tunnels could also be dug under busy roads so that toads can reach their breeding ponds safely without being run over by cars. However, it is most important that the rainforests, which are home to huge numbers of frogs and toads, should be protected from further destruction.

The Mallorcan midwife toad has been saved from extinction by the protection of its habitat.

frog and toad fact!

Just under 100 species of frogs and toads are now either extinct or about to become extinct. Another 200 species are endangered and at risk of extinction.

Signs now warn drivers to watch out for toads that may be crossing the road.

29

Life cycle of a frog

Frogs take about two years to reach full size and be ready to breed. A female frog lays eggs that hatch into tadpoles. These gradually develop through metamorphosis into adult frogs. Frogs live for several years in the wild. Pet frogs, however, live much longer. Poison arrow frogs can live for up to 17 years and horned frogs up to 12 years.

Egg

Young tadpole

Older tadpole

Adult

Glossary

algae plants that grow in water, with no true stems or leaves

camouflage a way of hiding, using colours or shapes that blend with the surroundings

continent a large land mass, such as North America or Australia

embryo an animal at its very earliest stages of development

endangered animals that may become extinct if something is not done to protect them

extinct no longer in existence, disappeared completely

gills feathery structures that an animal uses to breathe underwater

habitat the place in which an animal or plant lives

larva the growing stage between the egg and the adult

mammal an animal that gives birth to live young, rather than laying eggs. Female mammals produce milk to feed their young

metamorphosis the changes that take place in some animals between the larva and the adult stage

predator an animal that hunts other animals

prey an animal that is hunted by other animals

reptile an animal with a backbone and a scaly skin, such as a snake or crocodile

Index